From the desktop of Jeffrey Simmons

A vacation in Paris inspired Miroslav Sasek to create childrens travel guides to the big cities of the world. He brought me *This is Paris* in 1958 when I was publishing in London, and we soon followed up with *This is London*. Both books were enormously successful, and his simple vision grew to include more than a dozen books. Their amusing verse, coupled with bright and charming illustrations, made for a series unlike any other, and garnered Sasek (as we always called him) the international and popular acclaim he deserved.

I was thrilled to learn that *This is Texas* will once again find its rightful place on bookshelves. Sasek is no longer with us (and I have lost all contact with his family), but I am sure he would be delighted to know that a whole new generation of wide-eyed readers is being introduced to his whimsical, imaginative, and enchanting world.

Your name here

Published by arrangement with Simon & Schuster Books for Young Readers,
Simon & Schuster Children's Publishing Division

This edition first published in the United States of America in 2006 by
UNIVERSE PUBLISHING
A Division of Rizzoli International Publications, Inc.
300 Park Avenue South
New York, NY 10010
www.rizzoliusa.com

© Miroslav Sasek, 1967

*See updated Texas facts at end of book

2006 2007 2008 2009 2010 / 10 9 8 7 6 5 4 3 2 1

Printed in China

ISBN-10: 0-7893-1389-8
ISBN-13: 978-0-7893-1389-8

Library of Congress Control Number: 2005907352

Cover design: centerpointdesign

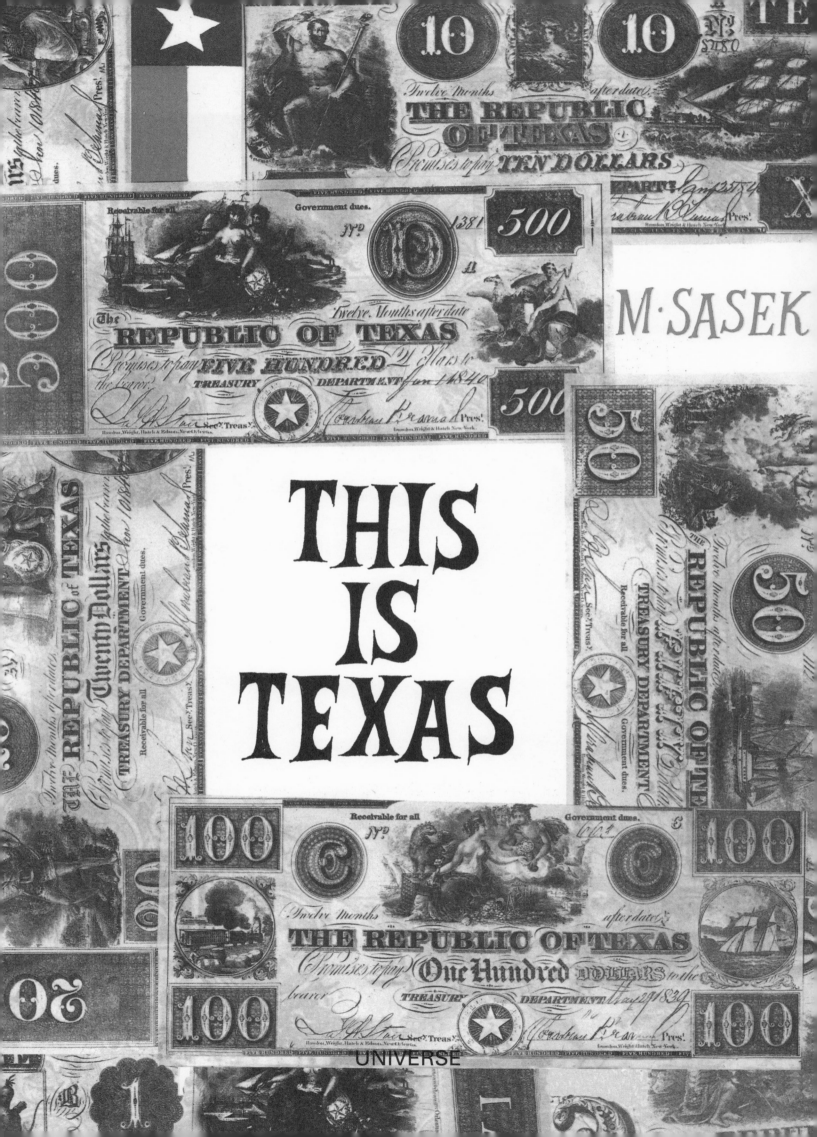

M·SASEK

THIS IS TEXAS

UNIVERSE

Texas, the Lone Star State, has 254 counties, 268,581 square miles, and 22 million friendly people. It was named for an Indian tribe, the Tejas, meaning "friends."
It was admitted to the Union in 1845 as the 28th state. The state motto is Friendship.

is the state flower —

the state tree is the pecan —

the state bird is the mockingbird —

the state song is *Texas, Our Texas*.

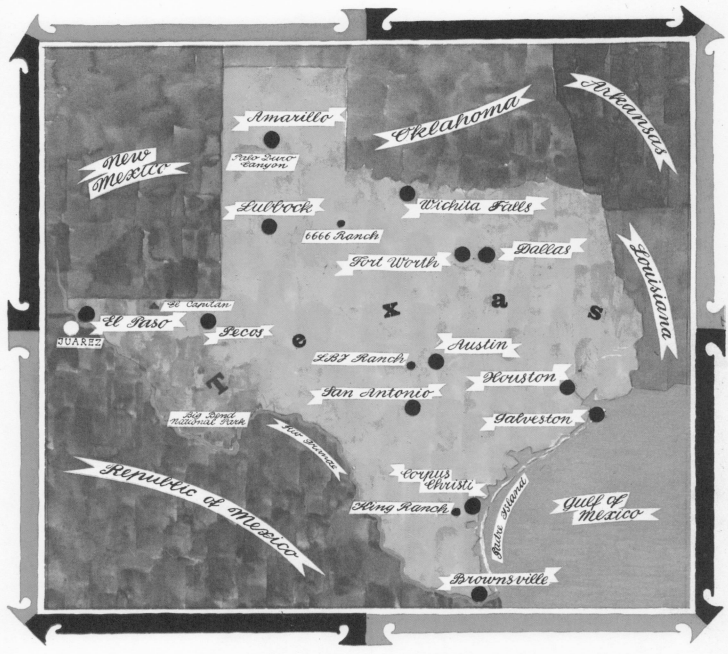

Texas is the biggest state in the United States[1]. It is a country in itself and a land apart.

Everything you see in Texas is one of the biggest in the universe or in the world or in the nation or at least in the county or, at any rate, the biggest in the town.

Texas is one of the nation's biggest producers of spinach, millionaires, and onions; it produces more oil, folk songs[2], cattle, carbon black, natural gas, and tall tales than any other state.*

[1] Except Alaska

[2] Except Tennessee

Texans wear the world's most uncomfortable boots and are known to be the world's worst walkers.

But who cares? In Wichita Falls everybody drives a Cadillac.*

Under the Stetsons —

different faces.

Under the Texas skies —

different landscapes.

Approaching the Rio Grande Valley

Grain elevators in the Panhandle

Stewart Beach in Galveston

Padre Island with its hundred miles of dunes

Palo Duro Canyon in the Panhandle
is named for the hardwood cedar
brush that grows there. Indians
made their bows and arrows with
this wood. The canyon is about 120
miles long. The settlers fought Indians
here and the early explorers and
pioneers crossed the canyon. So did
the Gold Rush miners on their way to
California. It is now a state park.

West of Pecos

El Capitan rises to 8,078 feet. It
was called Signal Peak by the early
pioneers because Indian lookouts
made signal fires on the top.

Different kinds of vegetation —

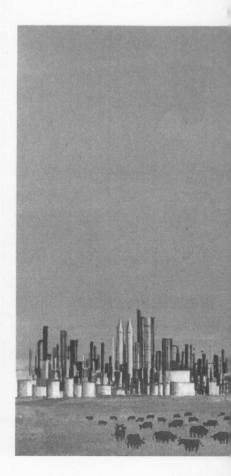

Botanic Gardens in Fort Worth with thousands of rosebushes, tens of thousands of plants of 2,500 different species, and more than twenty specialty gardens.

Pasadena, "The Land of Flowers" in Spanish, is a flowering suburb of Houston. Oil refineries, meat-processing establishments, and chemical and plastic plants sprout everywhere.

St. Mary's Cathedral in Galveston

Different kinds of architecture —

The largest cottonseed mill in the world in Lubbock

— and strange communities

Prairie Dog Town in Lubbock

Texas has the roomiest mobile houses —

the hairiest goats —

the best-shaved hogs —

the juiciest steaks —

the humpiest bulls —

the most statuesque cows —

the wildest wild turkeys.

Texas's wealth is said to be hanging from the trees, grazing on the grass, and stored under the ground. The conquistadores looked only for yellow gold in Texas — they did not yet know about the black gold.

The most familiar sight on the Texas landscape is the device for lifting oil to the surface, the pumping jack.

Sometimes they do not need the pumping jack at all: the oil is pushed to the surface by pressure.

Here is a farmer refueling his plane from his own oil well.

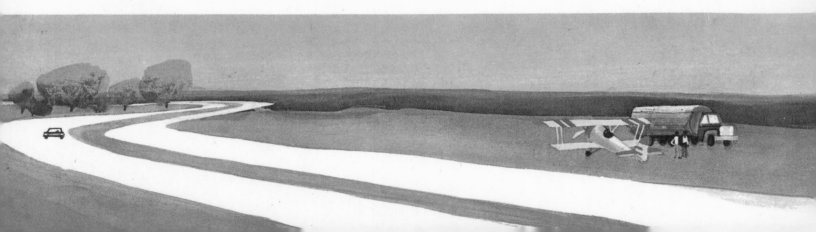

Nearly 250,000 oil wells are scattered across Texas and nearly 25 percent of all U.S. oil is produced there. Most Texas newspapers cover the oil industry.

Texas has about 30,000 private planes. And 1,430 private airports. This is NOT one of them.

Austin is the capital of Texas. Its site was selected in 1839 in the middle of Indian country and it was named for Stephen F. Austin, son of Moses Austin, the leader of the first American settlers in Texas. With its many offices and colleges, it is above all a city of politicians and scholars. Its present population is about 650,000.

Ancient oaks and architecture
of the period adorn the oldest section
of the city: the Bremond Block.

Texas capital's Capitol (309 feet) is seven feet taller
than the national capital's Capitol. It is built of pink
granite, and atop its dome stands the Goddess of Liberty.
Construction was completed in 1888.

Governor's Mansion
It has been the residence of all governors of the
state since 1856.

The Millet Opera House.
Built in 1878, it was once the
cultural focus of Austin. The
auditorium had 800 movable
seats. The Opera House was
in use until 1896.

Texas has some 130 universities and colleges. The University of Texas in Austin is the largest, with a campus population of 50,000. It was opened in 1883.

The rig of the Santa Rita No.1 oil well, discovered in 1923 on land belonging to the University of Texas in Reagan County. It is now on the campus — probably the only oil rig on academic soil anywhere.

Fort Worth — Where the West Begins

Fort Worth skyline

In about 150 years "Cowtown" Fort Worth has developed from a frontier post and cattle market into a modern industrial and cultural city, without losing its Western character. It won an All-America City Award in 1965 and 1993.

West 7th Street

This is Casa Mañana with its metal dome, the first musical theater-in-the-round in this country.

Leonard's Subway, the only privately owned subway in the world, takes you from the parking lot to Leonard's Department Store.* No charge. It is also the only subway in Texas where passengers might drown in oil.

Will Rogers Memorial Center features symphony orchestra concerts, fat livestock and horse shows, operas, and the world's largest indoor rodeo.*

Rodeo is Spanish for "roundup." The buck jumpers have a fairly easy life: they work for only ten seconds about twenty times a year.*

Six Flags is a $10 million amusement park between Fort Worth and Dallas. Texans have lived under six different flags. The Spaniards ruled the vast territory for more than 300 years from 1519. The French founded a short-lived colony in 1685 on Lavaca River — Fort St. Louis. When Mexico won its independence from Spain in 1821, Texas became part of the new country. After the Battle of San Jacinto, in 1836, Texas unfurled its own Lone Star flag and became a free republic. In 1845 Texas joined the United States. During the Civil War, Texans fought under the Confederate flag. Since then it has been the Stars and Stripes forever.

There are more than one hundred attractions in the Park.

Bank robbers about to bite the dust under a hail of bullets from the sheriff's gun —

Chaparral antique cars —

Mexican Fiesta Train* —

Hi, Big Joe!

On November 22, 1963, Elm Street in Dallas was the scene of the assassination of President John F. Kennedy. The cross marks the spot where the president was shot. The shots came from the window marked by the circle.

"Big D" for Dallas

It began as a trading post in 1841 and its first customers were the Caddo Indians. Now Dallas trades with the whole world. It is the financial hub of Texas and it has more banks and insurance companies than any other city in the state. It is a leader in culture and fashion, too.

33

The deposits in the banks of Dallas total $16 billion. And if you think that's enough and don't want to add to it, you can leave all your money at Neiman Marcus, one of the most elegant stores in the world.

Here is Big Tex with his seventy-five-gallon hat, the biggest Texan of them all, welcoming visitors at the State Fair of Texas, held in Fair Park.*

In Texas you'll find London, Paris, Athens, Moscow, Nazareth, Roma, and Milano — but no Venice. However, it has San Antonio with its gondolas on the San Antonio River.

San Antonio still retains some of the romantic charm
of Old Spain. With its eventful past and cosmopolitan
air, it is one of the most pleasant places in Texas.
Industry? Electronics, aircraft, oil, cattle, chili powder —
you name it. It is also the site of the Army's largest
military base and has more retired generals among its
residents than any other American town.*

The picturesque San Antonio River winds its way twenty
feet below street level through the heart of the city. The
river walk — Paseo del Rio — lined with tropical plants
and Mexican, Italian, and Chinese restaurants, takes
you to the unique Arneson Theater, where the audi-
ences, sitting on grassy seats on one bank, watches
the shows on a stage on the other bank of the river.

Governor's Palace, dated 1749, was the
official residence of Spanish governors. It is
the only example in Texas of early aristocrat-
ic Spanish residences.

The governor's office and bedroom

38

San Antonio bookstore

There is all you need if you want to start a long literary argument — or to end one quickly.*

But go easy on those fights. The lawmen are Texas-size, too.

Mission San José

Five of the eight old Spanish missions still standing in Texas are in San Antonio. A mission served as a church, hospital, school, fort, and an outpost of civil administration. The best-preserved mission in the United States is Mission San José, founded in 1720.

Here is the famous stone-carved rose window.

Mission San Antonio de Valero was founded in 1718,
two years earlier than Mission San José. The Alamo,
originally the mission's chapel, became the scene of one
of the most heroic battles in American history. During the
Texas-Mexican War, a band of 200 courageous men led
by William Travis and Jim Bowie was besieged there
by several thousand troops of the Mexican would-be
dictator Santa Anna. On the thirteenth day of the siege,
March 6, 1836, Santa Anna's troops stormed the Alamo
from all sides. In fierce man-to-man fighting that lasted
from dawn to dark every one of the defenders was killed.
Among them were the famous frontiersman Davy Crockett
and his volunteers from Tennessee.

Davy Crockett

43

Six weeks later, rallying his Texan forces, General Sam Houston appealed to his soldiers: "Remember the Alamo!" With this cry on their lips the 910 Texans defeated the Mexican forces of Santa Anna, numbering over 1,200. The battle of San Jacinto lasted eighteen minutes and won Texas its independence. Sam Houston became the first president of Texas, and "Remember the Alamo!" has been the Texans' battle cry ever since.

The San Jacinto Monument, 22 miles east of Houston, marks the battleground. It is 570 feet high, the world's tallest memorial column.

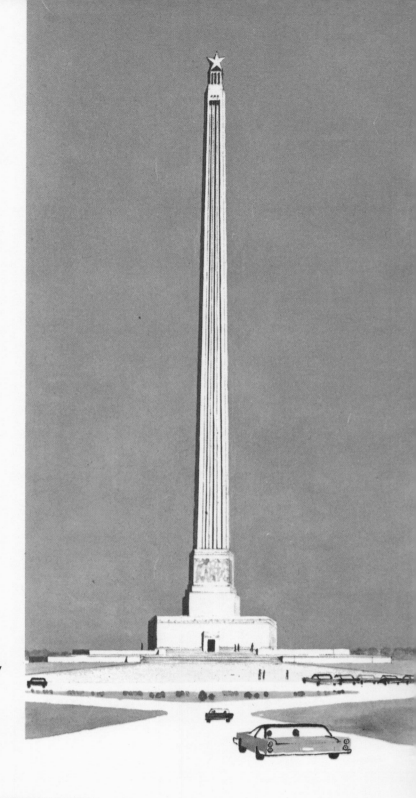

The San Jacinto battleground is now a state park. Moored there, not far from the Monument, is the battleship USS TEXAS, retired veteran of two world wars.

Who said Texans brag? This is a humble picture of Travis Street and Houston's tallest building — the Humble Building.*

HUMBLE BLDG

To say that every Texan is a millionaire is just a tiny little bit of an exaggeration. For instance, they have "only" 125,000 millionaires in Houston. And nearly two million non-millionaires.

The two Roman emperors who built the Colosseum would marvel at the sight of Houston's Astrodome. It is the world's first domed and air-conditioned sports stadium. Its ceiling is 208 feet high, its diameter is 710 feet. Parking is available for 30,000 cars.

Hey, Titus and Vespasianus, y'all watch this!

The Astrodome seats 52,000 for baseball, 62,000 for football, and 66,000 for boxing matches. The roof has 4,596 skylights letting in the sunlight needed to play day baseball.*

APOLLO
FULLSCAPE MOCKUP
OF PROJECT APOLLO
COMMAND MODULE

Once Texas was said to be so lawless that "not even the laws of gravity were obeyed there." And they still are not obeyed at NASA's Johnson Space Center, thirty miles from Houston. All U.S. space missions are directed from here. And so Houston, nicknamed Space City, was proud to be uttered by Neil Armstrong when he became the first man to walk on the moon on July 20, 1969.
Space Center Houston, the Official Visitors Center of Johnson Space Center, conducts daily tours and offers movies, interactive exhibits, and live shows and presentations.

Tent Maker Creek Canyon near
Amarillo in the Panhandle. See
the cowboy down there looking
for stray cattle? He works for
the Marsh Ranch and his name
is J.C. King.

There are a quarter of a million farms and
ranches in Texas. This is one of them.

Main gate

The Marsh Ranch has 10,000 acres, 500 mother cows, 20 bulls —

one longhorn —

and one cowboy: J.C. King.

The King County sheriff's residence in Guthrie (pop. 224).

The town is also the headquarters of the Four Sixes Ranch, one of the largest in Texas.

This is its branding iron.

But the largest ranch in Texas is the King Ranch in Kleberg County. With its 825,000 acres, King Ranch is 1,700 times larger than the principality of Monaco.

Main gate

There are 500 miles of roads on the ranch, and with its 2,000 miles of fencing, a fence could be built along the whole length of the Rio Grande. The ranch has 350 employees.

A 1910 stable fit for a king's horse. Now the ranch has about 500 horses and they wouldn't all fit in.

King Ranch has 65,000 head of cattle. The ranch developed the first breed of cattle originated in the Western Hemisphere — Santa Gertrudis, known to all cattlemen in the world.

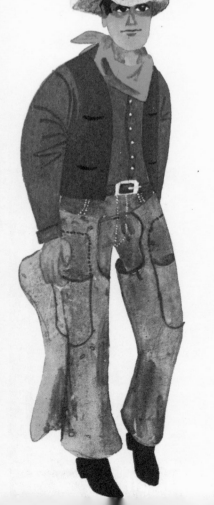

A cowboy may spend as little as ten dollars for his horse and as much as a thousand dollars for his saddle.

El Paso, formerly called El Paso del Norte, the lowest pass though the Rockies, was traveled by Indians, Spanish explorers, and gold seekers. El Paso and its Mexican sister-city, Juárez, are the two largest and oldest cities on the U.S.-Mexican border. Ysleta, an El Paso suburb, is the oldest town in Texas.

The world's only International Street-Car takes you from El Paso in the U.S. to Juárez in Mexico for only 10 cents.* But then, they are just across the Rio Grande from each other.

Juárez is the shopping paradise for American tourists as well as for the local Indians. Though many goods are different, the chewing gum tastes equally fine on both sides.

57

Rio Grande in Brownsville

Rio Grande does not look very "Grande." But what it lacks in width
it makes up in length: it is 1,896 miles long. It forms part of the
boundary between the U.S. and Mexico and both countries draw
water from it. The U.S. customhouse is on the left side of the
bridge, the Mexican on the right.

The Lower Rio Grande Valley produces the juiciest oranges in the world and the pinkest pink grapefruits. To say nothing of forty vegetable crops a year.

A song says that Texas was made by a devil who wanted a hell of his own. He made it out of sand and stones, and a generous mixture of cacti, coyotes, tarantulas, horned toads, and rattlesnakes.

Wouldn't he be surprised if he could see what happened when the Texans took over!

Corpus Christi — "The Door to Wonderland."

THIS IS TEXAS...TODAY!

* Page 7: Today Texas also produces more cotton, wool, mohair, and leather than any other state.

* Page 8: Today in Wichita Falls you will see more pickup trucks than Cadillacs.

* Page 28: Today Leonard's has become Tandy Center. The subway closed in 2002.

* Page 29: Today Reliant Stadium, in Houston, is home to the world's largest indoor rodeo.

* Page 29: Today buck jumpers are known as saddle broncs, and these cowboys would likely claim saddle bronc riding as the toughest rodeo event to master because of the timing, finesse, and technical skills required.

* Page 31: The Mexican Fiesta Train made its last run in 1978. In 1986 it was replaced by La Vibora ("The Viper"), a bobsled ride.

* Page 35: Today Big Tex wears a different outfit. He received a new wardrobe in 2002, when he turned 50 years old.

* Page 37: Today Fort Hood, outside of Austin, is the Army's largest national military base, and Virginia, followed by Texas, has more retired generals among its residents than any other state.

* Page 39: Today you'd be hard-pressed to find a bookstore in San Antonio, or anywhere in Texas, that sells guns.

* Page 45: Today Houston's tallest building is the JPMorgan Chase Tower.

* Page 46: Today the Astrodome, officially known as the Reliant Astrodome, is used for such events as concerts, high school and adult league sports games, and conferences. Houston's professional baseball team, the Astros, play in Minute Maid Park; the football team, the Houston Texans, play in Reliant Stadium; and boxing matches are held in Reliant Center.

* Page 56: Today the street car is not in operation. It stopped running in 1973.